ACING RACING

FRED FAOUR

ACING RACING

AN INTRODUCTORY GUIDE
TO HORSE GAMBLING FOR POKER PLAYERS,
SPORTS BETTORS AND ONLINE ACTION JUNKIES

outskirts
press
Denver, Colorado

TABLE OF CONTENTS

ACKNOWLEDGEMENTS

This book came together pretty quickly. When Black Friday crushed all of our poker dreams, it became apparent that there was a void to be filled. I believe horse racing can fill that void.

Several people are responsible for this book. My mother, Pat, from whom I inherited my degeneracy. My wonderful children, who put up with my love of gambling.

Also, my horse racing mentor, Scott Scully, the best handicapper I've ever known, and Rocket Rosen, my longtime gambling buddy.

Also, major thanks to Curt Meyer, a brilliant artist who did the cover for this, and Sam Houston Race Park for their betting tables. Special thanks to Eric Wing of the NTRA for his help and the Daily Racing Form for its assistance as well.

And finally, most of all, thanks to my awesome wife Valerie. This is for her.

CHAPTER ONE

INTRODUCTION

If you are reading this, chances are you are one of the hundreds of thousands of Americans who got stung by the government's crackdown on online poker.

You like to gamble. You enjoy the action. You loved the convenience of logging on and finding a game right away.

Yes, you like playing live, too, but it's not always easy to get to the casino or poker room. You need to replace that rush that came with multi-tabling and constant action.

Or maybe you are a sports gambler, but you have problems finding ways to wager legally.

You might also be a horseplayer looking for some new strategies and ways to increase your action. You like sitting at home watching TVG or HRTV and playing along with the hosts, getting bets on as many races as possible.

Maybe you are just a gambling degenerate who likes to get his/her wager on in a variety of ways.

This book is for all of you.

Let's face it; most people gamble for the action. Poker exploded in the mid-2000s, going from a backroom, shady collection of gamblers to a mainstream game played by everyone. ESPN made it into a national phenomenon, and sites like Pokerstars and Full Tilt made it cool to play cards.

It is a game that in many ways is a metaphor for life; it's you against the world. Sometimes you do everything right and lose. Sometimes you can do the wrong thing and come out ahead. In the end, if you do the right thing more often than not, it all evens out, and you come out ahead. It is skill with an element of luck thrown in, just like life.

Other casino games don't provide the same rush. In craps, blackjack, roulette -- it's you against the house, and the house always has an edge on every game. Sure, you get lucky every now and then, but long-term, you can't win. If you did, you would be the one owning the giant, lavish casino instead of visiting it.

There is one other form of gambling that is similar to poker. Like poker, the players place their wagers, the house takes its cut, and the players play each other for the rest.

Like poker, there are a variety of wagering opportunities. Like poker, it involves skill with an element of luck.

It is also perfectly legal to play online in the United States. There are some restrictions, and some states do not allow it, but chances are you can open an account today and begin legally wagering immediately.

Are you a tournament poker player? Many of these legal sites offer tournaments as well, and the skill it takes to win a poker tournament translates very well to winning the tournaments for this form of gambling.

Yes, horse racing offers almost everything poker does.

Unfortunately, it has much the same identity poker did before the online boom; shady old men wearing derbies and hanging in dark rooms. It is seen as a sport for the rich; beautiful ladies in big hats sipping on expensive drinks. Gamblers tend to find it too confusing to try to understand all the elements and nuances. The research seems difficult to figure out in order to have an edge over other players.

All of those are myths.

In truth, the live racing experience is a blast. But thanks to the online sites and cable channels that show you almost every race, you can do what you always did playing poker, too – stay at home, get all the action you want on your laptop and use all the same skills you've developed playing poker to make money.

What did you always hear about Hold 'Em? "A minute to learn, a lifetime to master?"

Horse racing isn't all that different. Once you understand the basics, you can apply your own poker and wagering skills and develop a strategy that works for you. Isn't that what you did with poker? Learn as much theory as possible and apply it to your own games?

You will learn that horse racing is the same thing. Each race is like a different hand in poker. How you play it will depend on your bankroll, position, and what the other players are doing.

The concept of this book is not to give you one strategy for playing. The idea here is to give you all the tools you need to get started, provide some high action strategy and theory, and do it in terminology you will understand from your poker life.

We'll also tell you where you can bet online, where you can watch the races, and provide strategies for action junkies as well as those who simply want to grind out a profit.

And don't worry; if you are a sports gambler, we've got strategies for you, too. Longtime horseplayers who are looking for ways to adjust to the online gambling world will find everything they are looking for here as well.

The idea is not to overload you. Many horse racing books delve so deeply into minutia they lose readers who are just trying to get started. The concept here is to give you a quick overview and basic understanding of the game. The idea is to have fun, not overwhelm you with thousands of wagering angles.

Once you are in, where you go from there will be up to you.

Simply put, this book should be your first step into a new gambling world, one that should satisfy all your needs.

If all that sounds appealing, read on. This book is for you.

CHAPTER TWO

THE BASICS

Horse racing is a terrific experience. Going to the race track is a blast, even if it is just for simulcasting. Hanging with a group, betting a variety of tracks and enjoying adult beverages simply adds to the experience. The majesty of live racing provides a thrill you can't get anywhere else.

Thanks to technology, you can simulate that experience at home, playing online. If you are a pure fan of the sport, there's nothing better than being at a track.

If you like action, online play is just as satisfying.

Much like poker, there are two key elements to horse racing:

Handicapping the race. This simply means going through past performances to learn the horses' histories, then determining which horses are most likely to do well.

To do this, you use the information provided to come up with the most logical outcome. This is essentially the same as playing a hand in poker; you make your best guess as to what the other players are holding and evaluate your hand in relation to those, then come up with the most logical result.

Wagering. Once you have made the determination, you have a wide variety of bets to choose from, hoping to maximize the value of the race. Sometimes, the right play is to pass the race (fold). Because you have so many wagering options, however, it is possible to play a greater number of races. As you get more skilled, you will learn how to do this. In the beginning, however, we offer a strategy that will give you a few strong scenarios to look for. In the online world, this should give you no shortage of options.

The next few chapters will focus on understanding the basics of horse racing: how races are set up, the different classes, how to read past performances and essentially how to select the most likely winners. Then we will focus on the different forms of wagering and how to choose which one fits each race. We will approach these wagers with the mindset of a poker player.

The terminology will be different, but we'll also give you a glossary of those terms. Once you are set, we will tell you where you can wager online legally.

THE RACES

Each horse race is different. A racetrack will card anywhere from eight to 10 races on a given day. Usually, you have 20-30 minutes or so between races to handicap. The smartest play is to do your handicapping of the races ahead of time, then adjust based on track conditions or changes (such as late scratches) throughout the day.

If you are playing online and want to hit as many tracks as possible, doing your work ahead of time also makes a big difference, and leaves you more time to focus on the wagers. If you are accustomed to playing several tables at once online, this is for you. (On a busy weekend, races will be coming every couple of minutes at tracks all around the country, so you can get all the action you want).

Races are usually entered several days in advance. Horse owners will consult with trainers and pick a race that best fits their horse.

Horses race for a set amount of money, called the purse. Quite simply, better horses run for more money than cheaper ones.

Each track generally publishes a program that contains basic information about the horses. Often these programs contain past performances, which are basically the history of the horse. It is not unlike having a record of every one of your opponents at the poker table.

There are several different types of horses that run; for our purposes, we will focus primarily on thoroughbreds, however many of the strategies will work for quarter horses and standardbreds as well as greyhounds.

There are also many different types and distances of races; at first these can seem confusing, but we have put them in a simple format that helps you understand the class levels.

Horses rarely run more than once every three weeks or so. If you follow the races long enough, you will become more familiar with the horses themselves, and as you watch more races, you will also get to know the different racetracks, jockeys and trainers better. Just like poker; the more you play, the more you will learn.

PAST PERFORMANCES

Frankly, playing the races without some form of past performances is like playing Hold 'Em with one card; you might get lucky and win a hand every now and then, but other players will always have the advantage. Remember, you are competing against other people, so each bit of information you can gather on a given race or a given horse gives you an edge. Just like in poker; the more understanding and information you have, the better your odds of beating your opponents.

The program gives you some basic information that will tell you about the horse. Eventually, we recommend using Daily Racing Form or Equibase past performances, which are much more intricate and provide greater information to help you make your best possible guesses.

The Daily Racing Form has been a staple for horseplayers forever. It is highly recommended. The best package for online players is the Formulator Past Performances, which provide detailed histories on every horse. For now, you should keep it simple, but when you are ready for the next step, give the Formulator package a try on drf.com.

A sample program page with past performances

appears on page 11.

Each horse is assigned a number. This will be the horse's wagering number. If you like horse No. 1, when you place your wager, you will use the number, not the name.

(Sometimes you will see a 1 and a 1A. This is essentially a two for one bet; you get both horses. If either wins, you win)

Each horse is also assigned morning-line odds. These odds are not fixed, as in sports betting, but they are merely a guess on the part of the track handicapper as to how the public will wager.

Keep in mind that horse racing is pari-mutuel wagering, meaning the odds will change based on the size of the wagering pools. All gamblers are betting into the same pools and collecting their winnings from those who lose.

The morning-line odds are designed to give you an idea on what horses the public is most likely to wager on. They are useful in terms of looking for value.

The morning-line favorite is the horse assigned the lowest odds before wagers begin. Favorites win roughly 33 percent in horse racing, so the bulk of our wagering strategies will focus on the other 67 percent.

When reading the program, keep in mind the morning line is simply how they think the public will play. It's not unlike an early betting line in sports. The difference is you can lock in your sports bet at those odds; in horse racing, it all depends on how the public bets. If you wager on a horse that is 5-1 when you bet and the horse goes off 2-1 in the final odds, you get 2-1, not 5-1. This can frustrate a sports bettor, but keep in mind that it can also go the other way and you can wind up with superior odds at post time than what you initially bet.

Those numbers are important to understanding racing. Odds are simply the return based on a percentage of the wagering pool.

Distance of a race is also important. Races are anywhere from as short as four furlongs (a furlong is an eight of a mile or 220 yards) to a mile and a half. Some horses are better sprinting at the short races, while others are "route" horses and enjoy going long. Truly outstanding horses are good at both.

In addition to figuring out the best horses at the best level, you will also have to speculate on which horses will run best at the given distance. (The Kentucky Derby, America's most popular race, is run at 1 ¼ miles).

On top of that, some horses are "horses for courses" that like certain racetracks. All of this will come into play in your handicapping.

It sounds like a lot to learn and it can be confusing. But it's really very simple, and all of that information is available on the page we are about to show you, and all of it can be easily applied to your wagering decisions.

The next page provides you with a basic explanation of what everything means:

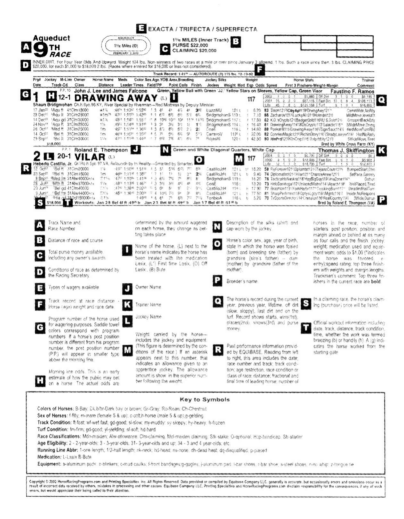

Each line is read across. It is basically a history of the horse's career. It paints a picture of where each horse is in the race. Take some time to familiarize yourself with these past performances; when you move on to multiple track betting, the ability to sort through these quickly is a major advantage.

There is a lot of information here; determining what is important and what can be tossed isn't always easy. The key elements to focus on are a) Who the horse ran against; b) how the horse did against that company; c) how fast the horse actually can run; and d) How did the pace scenario impact the race?

The big question then becomes how will the horse run today?

We tend to focus primarily on the class of the race a horse is best suited for and when it has turned in its peak efforts. If a horse consistently wins for $5,000 claiming, then struggles for $10,000, he will likely return to form when he drops back to the lower level.

Our strategy focuses on the basic premise that every horse is capable of winning the race. Then we begin a process of elimination to determine the most likely to run fourth, then third, then second, then first. From there we determine how many horses can actually be played and how the race should be approached.

Our recommendation is to use the Daily Racing Form past performances, either by purchasing the Form or buying online at drf.com. The following page (courtesy of the Daily Racing Form) explains in detail the past performances as they appear in the Form.

The Form's past performances will give you a significant edge over other players, especially the Beyer Speed Figures, which you will read more about later.

Now you have a sense of the basics and are ready to proceed. First, however, it is important to understand one of the key elements of horse racing – the oft-mis-used term "class."

CLASS

The term "class" is often overused in horse racing, but its basic premise is that it represents the quality of a horse based on the caliber of its competition. Let's say Horse A wins its last race by seven lengths. Horse B finished second in his last race by 20 lengths. Does that automatically mean Horse A is better?

Put it in human terms. If Donald Driver ran a sprint against Ussain Bolt, he would get crushed. If Aaron Rodgers beat B.J. Raji by an equal margin, does that mean he would beat Driver? (Look, the Packers won the Super Bowl. Plug in your own team's guys and it works out the same).

Of course he wouldn't. So determining the quality of those races is paramount to understanding the basic fundamentals of horse racing.

Each race is designated as a certain type in order to try to fairly balance the races. In addition, what track a horse runs at often helps define its class. The better horses run where there is more money. More on that later. For now, here are the types of races:

Maiden races: For horses that have yet to win a race. There are high-dollar maiden races for promising horses often called "maiden allowance" races. These races often produce horses that go on to become great. In poker parlance, these are suited connectors. Many times they lead to monster hands. Sometimes they lead to absolutely nothing. There are also maiden claiming races for cheaper horses with lesser futures. See the claiming races below for a more detailed explanation.

Claiming races: This is the bread and butter of most race tracks, especially the lower levels. Claiming races carry a certain price tag. For instance, if a race is a $10,000 claiming race, every horse entered can be purchased by anyone with a license for $10,000. The idea is you won't put a really good horse in for a smaller price, because someone might purchase it. By contrast, if your horse is most successful running for a $5,000 claiming price, you won't run it for $20,000, because it will likely be facing much better horses. This is the majority of races, and in poker terms, they can be any random hand. Catch the right flop and you can cash, but you could be in against anything.

Allowance races: Most of these races are for talented up and coming horses. Most really good horses will go through what is called *conditions* on their way to a career racing against the best. These conditions often appear in allowance races as "non-winners of two races" or "non-winners of three races," etc. There are many conditions within the allowance races and many class levels, which we will break down in more detail later. In general, most allowance races are the racing equivalent of pocket 8s or 7s; certainly worth seeing a flop.

Stakes races: Now we are getting in to the premium hands. Stakes races are for the very best horses. Like the other forms, there are divisions within the stakes. A Grade I Stakes is essentially pocket aces – theoretically, the best of the best, like the Kentucky Derby or Breeders' Cup Classic.

Not all maiden, allowance, claiming and stakes races are created the same. There are divisions within those as well, such as horses that have never won two races, or three races, or haven't won a certain amount of races in a year.

Think of all of these in terms of starting hands and you will get a sense of the quality; it doesn't mean a good claiming horse won't beat a stakes horse on a given day; after all, your aces can get cracked by pocket 3s sometimes. But at least you have a general understanding of the basics as you move forward in your handicapping career.

SPEED

Horse racing isn't as simple as which horse runs the fastest. It is a combination of the class breakdowns detailed above, plus the pace of a given race and the final time.

Some horses love running shorter races and are most effective. These horses – called sprinters – usually race

5-7 furlongs, depending on the track.

Route horses prefer longer races, usually one mile and over.

Horses are also by nature pack animals; some will run better when they are in front by themselves. When pressured, they often wilt. Still others will run even better under pressure.

Go back to your sample past performances and notice the fractional times for each horse. This represents how fast the leader ran in each race. If the first quarter mile was run in :22, that was the speed run by the horse in the lead at that point.

The general standard is five lengths equals one second, so if a horse was one length behind at that point, his fractional time would be estimated at :22.20. A length is roughly the length of a horse. All of this is subject to interpretation by chart callers who record the races, so there is always some wiggle room here.

Regardless, there is an old saying that pace makes the race, and that is often true. A horse that makes an easy lead under no pressure might run the best and fastest race of his life. That doesn't mean he will repeat it in a more difficult circumstance. It doesn't mean he won't, either, but it's important to look at the whys as much as the result.

We will break down pace later, but the best and easiest way to measure how fast a horse runs is speed figures. Depending on what type of past performance you purchase, it is usually the number in dark black. (We religiously use the Beyer Speed Figures in the Daily Racing Form and highly recommend them. See the detailed breakdown on Page 13).

It gives you an interpretive number on how fast the race actually went. Breaking things down to their most basic, using the speed figures will save you the work of breaking down final times yourself, and if betting multiple tracks is your plan, this is a must.

Combining the speed figures with the class of a race will narrow down your choices considerably.

In racing's simplest form, this will give you a starting point. From here, you can add more factors. Quite simply, this is like playing premium hands only while you learn to play poker. As these pages go on, we will expand what hands you play and the knowledge of the game itself. This basic understanding alone, however, will cash you some tickets.

CHAPTER THREE

JOCKEYS AND TRAINERS

There is a human factor in horse racing; trainers spend every day with their horses, preparing them to race. Good trainers put their horses in position to win more often than bad trainers.

Some trainers will also be owners who have one or two horses. They are essentially part timers; some are very good and can focus on their limited number of horses. Some are simply hobbyists.

Other trainers have massive stables, big money owners and deep pockets. It sounds simple, but the best trainers win the most races. They also generally get overbet. A shrewd player will figure out when it makes the most sense to bet against these trainers.

The Daily Racing Form has extensive trainer stats; once you start playing seriously, it's worth buying their Formulator package to get more detailed statistics on the types of races they do well in.

Every track has a dominant trainer; some have several. Excellent trainers can win up to 25 percent of their races. The good news is they still lose 75 percent, so you can make money off them.

Before you play a track, you should study who the top trainers are. Leading trainer standings are available at all tracks, usually online. Do not underestimate the importance of a shrewd trainer. It's not just that their horses are better, it's that they know where they belong and put them in the right races.

Jockeys, too, can have an impact. Again, it sounds simplistic, but the best riders get the best horses. They win at a higher percentage than other riders. In truth, the vast majority of races are won by a small percentage of riders.

Good jockeys, like good trainers, can also be bet against. They usually get a fan following and take more action when they are highly successful.

One good angle to look for is a successful jockey getting on a horse for the first time that has been ridden by lesser pilots. A good jockey won't necessarily improve a horse, but a bad jockey will slow a horse down. When a good jockey gets on that horse, the improvement comes from the bad jockey getting off the horse.

A bad jockey can cost you more money than two or three ex-wives combined.

Jockeys are better athletes than you might realize. They are smaller humans – usually around 115 pounds – who have to guide one-ton animals in tight quarters. They have to make split-second decisions during the course of a race that could not only mean the difference between winning and losing, but also possible injury or even death.

The stronger jockeys get their horses in the best

position to win. Lesser jockeys are often just trying to stay out of trouble. In addition, some jockeys simply get hot and win races in spurts. It's always a good idea to ride a hot jockey.

Low-percentage riders can be played if they are on a horse that can make an easy lead and coast along. Otherwise, they simply have to get lucky to win. These percentages for jockeys and trainers are something a poker player can understand. You are going to play high-percentage hands more often; you will also find ways to make lower percentage hands work in the right situations. That's all you are doing with trainers and jockeys; playing percentages and making your best possible guess.

CHAPTER FOUR

UNDERSTANDING ODDS

Poker players understand their odds. They know what their percentages are before they make a play.

Horse racing odds are even easier to understand.

The odds that appear on a tote board next to a horse's number reflect a percentage of money wagered. Because horse racing is pari-mutuel – meaning players against players – all money wagered goes into specific pools.

You cannot win more money than what is in the pool, just like you can't scoop more than what is in the pot in poker.

Each bet has an impact on the odds to reflect that percentage of the pool. Remember, you are not betting against the house, but against other players, with the house taking a rake, just like in poker.

Let's say you are Player A, and you have $500 to spend. Player B has $2.

It is a two-horse race. You bet your $500 on horse No. 1 Player B bets his $2 on horse No. 2.

Horse No. 2 wins. Player B collects $502 (minus the rake). You are out of luck.

If your horse wins, you also collect $502. So you risked $500 to win $2. Now multiply this by the hundreds of players at the track spreading their money throughout many horses, and your wagering pools develop.

The odds you see on a tote board reflect the horse's odds to win. All are based on a $2 wager.

So a horse that is 6-1 would return $14 (6 times the bet plus the initial $2 wager returned).

As a general rule, higher priced horses will also pay more in what is called the exotic wagers – trifectas, exactas, etc.

As we mentioned, favorites win 33 percent of the time, so we focus on the other 67 percent of the races and look for value in our bets, especially when playing a high volume of races online.

When you buy a program online or at the track, you will see odds next to a horse's name. These are the morning-line odds. As you read earlier, they basically represent what the track handicapper thinks the horse's win odds will be when actual wagering starts. Usually they know what they are doing, but many factors can move the odds. A trainer might be telling everyone who will listen that his horse is better than that. Rain might have changed track conditions. The track handicapper might have simply been way off.

So a horse might be 10-1 morning line, but if the public loves him and bets the majority of the pool on him, his actual odds might be 2-1. You will get paid off on the final odds once the race is run, so there might be some fluctuation up or down based on late wagers.

Your bet changes the pool, much as if you made a

huge sports wager and changed the line. Large volume wagers will decrease your win odds almost everywhere except at the biggest tracks, which have the most money in the pools.

The odds in horse racing are very simple to understand, and as you advance, you will realize that long shots are the best way to play. You only have to be right once out of ten races to break even if you are betting horses that are odds of 10-1 or higher. If you hit at a 20 percent level, you are making a profit.

Meanwhile if you are betting even money shots all day, you have to win 6 out of 10 in order to make a meager profit. We'll show you how to parlay these long shots into exotic wagers and massive payoffs.

CHAPTER FIVE

CHOOSING YOUR BETS
LIKE A POKER PLAYER

One advantage that horse racing has over other forms of gambling is a wide variety of wagers. You can play conservative wagers that are low-risk low-return, or you can swing for the fences at higher risk wagers that can bring you bigger scores.

Knowing which wager to choose for a given race is the key to success. If you lock in and simply play the same bets the same way every race, you are eventually doomed to failure, just as if you play your cards the exact same way every time you get them in poker.

The real art of horse racing is knowing how to bet once you have determined which horses you are playing.

If you are a creative post-flop poker player, you should thrive at this part of the game.

Later on, we'll give you a ranking system that will determine how much of your bankroll to risk, but for now, let's work on the basic forms of wagering:

WIN/PLACE/SHOW: Win, place and show wagers are the simplest form of betting in horse racing. A win bet is basically you betting on a horse to win the race. The minimum wager is $2, and the return will be based on the horse's final odds. If the horse is 5-1, you will get back $12 for your wager – your winnings plus your investment.

A place bet means you are betting on a horse to run at least second. If the horse wins or runs second, you get paid on your place bet based on a $2 wager. A show bet, the safest of all, is a bet on a horse to run third. The horse can finish first, second or third and you will get paid the show payoff. It is the lowest reward bet, but also the lowest risk.

Betting "across the board," means to bet a horse to win, place and show. If you are betting $2 across, it will cost you $6, because you are making three bets. If your horse wins, you collect on all three. If it runs second or third, you collect a smaller portion. This is a nice, safe way to get the hang of wagering without risking much.

For your first-ever bets, this is the safest way to go. We generally don't recommend across the board wagers on any horse not paying at least 4-1 to win.

QUINELLAS: Quinellas are not offered at every track, but they are a nice inexpensive way to play the races. A quinella means you are picking the first and second place horses in either order. In other words, if you like the 6 and 9 horses, you would buy a $2 quinella 6-9. If the race finishes 6-9 OR 9-6, you win.

A good beginner bet is the quinella box. This involves a minimum of three horses. From the example above, let's say you also like the No. 1 horse.

If you bet a $2 quinella box 1-6-9, your cost would be $6, because you are buying three combinations: 1-6, 1-9 and 6-9.

Any two of these three can finish 1-2, and you win.

Quinella boxes are very good beginner bets. They require a small outlay, and the returns can be solid. However, when betting quinella boxes with three horses, make sure at least one offers odds of 6-1 or higher. Betting quinella boxes with the top three favorites is the quickest way to go broke. You can also bet four and five horse quinella boxes. These give you more options to win, but also lessen the return. There are times to do this – four-horse quinella boxes in big fields where all of your horses are 8-1 or higher in odds, for instance – but for a beginner, start with three horses until you hit a few.

EXACTAS: The exacta wager is much like the quinella, only as the name suggests, you have to get the horses in the exact order. So if you bet a $2 exacta 6-9, it has to finish 6-9 for you to win. A 9-6 finish is a loss. Almost every track offers exacta wagering.

Here's where it gets a little confusing; you can also bet exacta boxes. Most tracks offer $1 minimum on these, so essentially a $1 exacta box is the same bet as a $2 quinella.

For instance, if you are boxing the 6 and 9, meaning they can finish in either order, a $1 box wager will cost you $2. You are buying two combinations, 6-9 and 9-6, and they can finish in either order. It is the same as a quinella wager.

A three-horse exacta box for a dollar will also cost you $6. (See the tables at the end of this chapter for box costs).

This is another low-risk, high-reward wager. It's an excellent way for beginners or those playing lots of races to get in some high action bets.

For poker players, the amount you wager should be in direct proportion to your bankroll (or chip stack, if you will). More on that in a bit.

TRIFECTAS: This is a bet that can bring you a huge return for a relatively small investment. A trifecta is the next step; you are attempting to pick the first three finishers in order. If you like the 1, 6 and 9 horses and place a trifecta wager 1-6-9, then the race has to finish in exactly that order.

This bet is an action junkies dream. The returns can often be hundreds or even thousands of dollars. The outlays can vary, and there are a myriad of strategies. Later on, we'll give you details on some spread plays that can yield outstanding returns.

However, for a beginner, sticking with the box concept is a good way to get started in trifectas. A $1 box 1-6-9 will cost you only $6. As with the other bets, they can finish in any order – 1-6-9, 1-9-6, 6-1-9, 6-9-1, 9-1-6, 9-6-1.

It is costing you $6 because there are six combinations in the box. A four-horse box will cost you $24 (24 combinations). For instance, adding the 4 horse and doing a 1-4-6-9 box will cost you that amount. Again, you only need three of the four to finish 1-2-3 in ANY order.

Boxing trifectas can bring big returns. Five-horse boxes are $60; but again, the more you wager, the more of a return you need. Boxing horses means not using all the favorites, or else you are simply throwing your money away. Good poker players won't make bets that will long term bring them losses. Boxes can work, but there needs to be long shots in the bet.

As with many of these bets, the best ones involve races where you feel you can leave out the favorite. These are your highest return bets. It's not always practical to do it, but as you will find later on, it is the fastest way to big profits.

Horses are consistently inconsistent; the cheaper the horse, the more likely it is to be unable to put together several big efforts in a row. These are good horses to bet against, especially in trifectas.

One issue with trifectas is you don't always know what your payoff is going to be. You will get paid based on how many people in the pool hit the bet.

SUPERFECTAS: This is one of the highest-yield bets in racing. It is also one of the most difficult. It requires picking four horses in exact order. Playing this bet straight is pretty much like playing a lottery ticket or trying to catch a one-outer on the river. It happens, but your odds are pretty low. Trying to make it happen on a regular basis is a fast way to the poor house.

Boxes are OK, but only if you have a significant bankroll. A four-horse box costs you $24, but you are trying to hit a four-outer on the river. In essence, all four of your horses have to run well in order for you to hit the bet. A five-horse box costs you $120 on a $1 base wager. So it can get pricey.

However, many tracks offer superfectas with a .10 minimum. These offer opportunities to pull some decent returns without spending as much money. Our preferred strategy for this involves wheeling, which we will discuss in detail later in the book.

DAILY DOUBLE: One of the oldest bets in racing, it involves picking the winner of two consecutive races (usually the first two and last two).

Old-timers love this bet. Pick threes and pick fours offer more value and return, however.

PICK THREE: This is pretty simple: it involves picking the winners of three consecutive races. Most often, it is based on a $1 wager.

Our favorite strategy in a pick three is to make a stand in one race, then spread deeper in the second and third races.

For instance, in race 1, let's say we like the 2 and the 3 horses. In race 2, we like the 5, 7, 8 and 9. And in the third we like 1, 3, 7, 9, 10.

The cost of this wager based on a $1 ticket would be $40. The math is simple: two horses times four horses times five horses. (2X4X5).

In a pick three, it is OK to use favorites, but you are likely not going to get much of a return unless you beat the favorite in two of the three races. When you have a race with a very heavy, odds-on favorite, it's only wise to play the pick three against this horse if you believe that the horse is a vulnerable favorite. The heavier favorites you beat, the better the return.

PICK FOUR: One of our favorite wagers; this is the same basic wager as a pick three, except it obviously involves four consecutive races. As with the pick three, if you make a stand in one race, you can spread out in the other three. Remember, big payoffs come from long shots winning; those returns increase exponentially in wagers like the pick four and superfecta.

From a poker standpoint, this is the equivalent of getting however many chips you are wagering in a multiplayer pot. Unlike poker, your returns are instant. You can pull a $1,000 score with $20 or $30. It is like winning a multi-table tournament in a matter of minutes.

For action junkies who advance past the basics, our recommended wagers are the trifecta, pick three, pick four and superfecta.

Later in the book we will give you some detailed strategies for playing these bets looking for big scores.

PICK SIX: Hitting a pick six can be a life-changing score. It is usually offered at big tracks with lots of money wagered. It is a $2 minimum wager, so trying to hit it can get expensive. The returns can be several hundred thousand dollars at times.

As the name would suggest, you must pick the winner of six consecutive races. If the bet does not get hit by someone, it carries over to the next day. Several-day carryovers at big tracks can create opportunities for massive scores.

However, it is an expensive bet. To simply have two horses in each race costs $128, so you have to have a bankroll to do it. If you can hit it for $32, so can the rest of the world.

Playing a pick six with a small bankroll is like sitting in on a $30/$60 game with a $200 bankroll; you have very little chance.

However, once you have progressed past the basics and have built up a bankroll, it's a bet to consider long term.

There are other wagers – Super High Fives (where you pick the top five finishers) pick 5s, etc. The basics are the same.

Now, the key to any race is selecting which wager to make for a given race. It is the same as deciding how to play a hand based on position, bankroll, etc.

For beginners, the safe plays are win/place/show and quinellas and exactas. As your handicapping skills develop, you can expand your game to trifectas, superfectas, pick threes and pick fours.

One good rule to keep in mind is to manage your

bankroll based on how many races you intend to play. One advantage over poker is you get to see your hands before you play them. You can do the handicapping ahead of time, so you can know which ones you plan to play in advance.

That's why it is critical – especially in the online world – to do your homework ahead of time. That way you can decide on the hands (races) you plan to pass on in advance, and focus on the wagers themselves when the races begin.

Bankroll management is a big key when you plan to play a significant amount of races. You should base your wagers on a 10 percent system; if you plan to bet 10 races, your average wager should be 10 percent of your total bankroll. If it's 100 races, it should be one percent. For races you have more confidence in, increase the percentage; for lesser races, decrease it. If you get ahead, you increase your wagers but still base them on 10 percent. If you get behind you decrease them.

For instance, you have a $100 bankroll for a 10-race card. You have found you like the third, sixth and ninth races the best but plan to bet all of the races. You don't like the first and second race as much.

You should average $10 per bet. For the races you like, double that to $20. For the ones you don't, drop it to $2 or $5. For the neutral ones, keep it at $10.

If you get a big score early and your bankroll is now $500, you can increase the wagers to a $50 average as opposed to a $10.

Often, after a score, it is wise to pull back your initial investment plus 10 percent, so you are guaranteed a profit for the day. Then base your wagers on 10 percent of the remaining bankroll.

Each race card is different. Each race is different. As in poker, you have many choices. Knowing how to make those choices – as in poker – separates the good players from the bad ones.

CHAPTER SIX

THE ONLINE GAME

As much as online poker changed the game, online horse wagering has changed that betting as well. You now have access to almost every track, constant action and an ability to pick and choose sites, races and situations that best fit your game.

The action can be fast and furious. If you liked playing several tables at once, you can do the same thing with horse racing.

On a weekend especially, races will come at you every couple of minutes. They key is patience, much like poker. Consider every race as a different game. Some are the equivalent of seven-card stud; some are limit, some no-limit. As with poker, you want to spend some time learning which game you are best at – or which types of races.

If you are better at turf sprints, you want to focus the bulk of your bankroll on those and spend lesser amounts on races you are less successful at. Chart your results; many sites will give you detailed results on your bets, so you can chart your more successful ones and the ones you are less successful on. Almost everyone will develop a type of race they are most comfortable and successful playing.

Online horse wagering allows you to do that. It is also perfectly legal. The key is to pick the right site. There are several really good ones. Some states have restrictions, however, so make sure you can legally wager in your state.

Here are some of our favorite legal online wagering sites:

Twinspires.com. Owned by Churchill Downs, it offers a varied wagering menu, excellent bonuses and a very user oriented site. An excellent place to play.

The big advantage is you get Churchill Downs. Some sites do not have access to Churchill, and if you enjoy playing that track, this is your site.

The customer service is very good, too. They understand horse players and are very responsive.

Betamerica.com. One of the most user friendly sites, it offers video on every track in addition to wagering services. They also offer tournaments as well as straight wagering. The wagering software is easy to use, and payoffs and deposits are quick and convenient. They also have an excellent rewards program. A very solid site.

The only negative is the wagering software can be tricky for multiple trifecta and superfecta wagers. It takes a little longer to get bets in using multiple horses than some other sites. That's no problem if you give yourself a little extra time. You also will need to take some time with the wagering software to figure that out.

Also, there is a slight delay on the videos, so it might

show horses in the starting gate, but it is too late to wager. As long as you know that going in, it's not a problem at all.

We are big fans of this site.

DRFbets.com (Xpressbet). Another very easy to use site, and one that also offers video of race tracks and tournaments. The rewards aren't as good as most other sites but you can get free past performances with certain amounts wagered, which are very helpful. There are some tracks they don't have access to (most notably Churchill Downs) but on the whole they are solid.

One big advantage is that the software is very easy for multiple wagers. If you are a big trifecta key player, you will figure out very quickly that you can go back to your original online template and move horses around quickly to make your bets much faster.

We use this site often and find it extremely solid.

TVG.com. An excellent site with good rewards and nice tie-in with an excellent TV production. Still not available in some states (most notably, Texas) but we highly recommend it. Tied in with the TV network, the overall experience is strong.

The main page also has all of the hosts' plays, so you can follow along with them if you don't get the races handicapped yourself.

The actual network TV coverage is terrific, especially for Los Alamitos if you need to get your night racing fix.

Racingchannel.com. Another solid site that isn't as advanced as some of the others, but it is still very easy to use. It's readily available and one that does a nice job of separating the types of races (thoroughbreds, standardbreds and greyhounds) and is easy to follow.

Horseplayerinteractive/hpi.com (Canada only). This is an excellent site for Canadians. Unfortunately, if you are in the U.S., you can't use it. But if you are in Canada, this is the place to play.

The software is easy to use and follow, and it offers easy access to potential payoffs for all wagers. The rewards are solid and it also provides access to live video so you can watch while you play. If you wind up living north of the border, you won't be disappointed in this site.

There are many others to choose from, but we have used all of these sites and feel comfortable recommending them. There are other sites tied to casinos and sports books such as Bodog and Betus, but make sure these are legal sites before wagering with them. We have had issues in the past with both, and since we all got burned by Black Friday, we only feel comfortable sending you to sites that are licensed and legal in the United State. Frankly, that is the entire point of this book. So any of the six listed above fit that criteria and are what we recommend.

The key is to find a site with easy deposits and withdrawals, excellent software and solid rewards for your wagers. All of these sites do that very well.

Once you have found one, it is critical to find a site that fits your personal needs. We recommend shopping around for the best bonuses, especially if you are a high volume player.

It's not just that you want a site where you can wager legally, you want one where you are comfortable navigating the software for your wagers.

For current horseplayers, the trick is learning how to get your bets done quickly and efficiently online. Poker players already know how to learn software before they begin playing for real, but many horseplayers are still very new to this. For you, it is much like using a self-service terminal at the racetrack. You make your own wagers and you also make your own mistakes. With all of these sites, we can't emphasize it enough: Spend some time with some small, easy wagers to learn how each site works. Know when your bet is official and know exactly how many steps you have to go through. That way, when you start playing multiple tracks in a short time frame, you know exactly what to do.

Another thing to look for is using multiple sites at once. In some cases, you will want to do this simply to allow access to one track you can't get on another site. Make sure you differentiate the steps between the two, because no two sites are alike.

It's easy to get caught up in the action and make mistakes, but if you spend some time before you get crazy, you will be much better off.

CHAPTER SEVEN

TOURNAMENTS

There is tournament play in horse racing, much like there is in poker. The best sites all offer some form of tournament, especially on weekends.

Some are based on real money, while others are based on virtual wagers; whoever has the most virtual wagers wins.

As in poker, a tournament strategy should be approached differently than a cash game.

For one thing, in tournaments, most of your wagering opportunities are limited. The bulk of tournaments will allow only win/place wagering, and cap maximum payoffs to keep someone from winning with one obscene long shot. While some also offer exotic wagering, the capped win/place is the most common form, and also that practiced in the NTRA's National Championship.

As in a poker tournament, it's usually a fixed buy-in, with payoffs based on results. Since that isn't always the case, this might sound simple, but make sure you read the rules. This will have a huge impact on how you approach your wagers.

The strategies for tournaments require you to have more winnings than the other players. The best way to accomplish this is to focus on horses that are no shorter than 8-1 in the wagering.

A standard tournament might feature 20 races at various tracks; 10 of the races will be mandatory – selected by the tournament committee – while 10 will be optional, where the player selects from a collection of race tracks.

Both sets of races require different strategies.

MANDATORY RACES

The mandatory races are the ones everyone bets. Picking the winners of these races is important, but not critical unless a long shot hits.

You won't gain much ground with a 4-5 shot. You should always play against short-priced favorites; often your long shot might pay as much to place as an odds-on winner. You don't need to get silly and chase complete bombs, but a steady diet of 6-1 to 10-1 shots will build your bankroll effectively and help put some distance between you and the other players.

As in poker, keeping an eye on the chip stacks is important. If you are woefully behind, you will need to do the equivalent of shoving all in, which is basically find the 20-1 shot with the best chance of winning. You might not like the horse at all, but a 4-1 winner does you no good in that situation.

Conversely, if you are well ahead and protecting your lead, getting winners is important, but with a really big lead, focusing on the only horses that can beat you – massive long shots – makes sense too. It all depends on how many races are left, your bankroll vs. the stacks of other players and how wide open the race actually is. With a solid lead, just making sure you have the winner is enough to stay on top, even if that horse is not long odds. But if you feel a favorite is vulnerable, protecting against the big score is the way to go.

Keep in mind the players chasing you will likely be focusing on long shots, so playing the favorite might pick them off, but it better be a strong favorite. A loss will almost certainly let another player pass you unless you have a massive lead.

This is standard poker tournament strategy; know your opponents and their chip stacks as well as your own.

The mandatory races late in a tournament will be critical.

Our favorite strategy is trying to build a chip stack early; catch a long shot in one of the early mandatory races and get your bankroll going. Then you can afford to be aggressive throughout, because you have room for error, just as you would in a poker tournament.

Playing short prices will not win a tournament, any more than waiting for premium hands will win you a poker tournament. You have to take high risk, high reward swings, especially in mandatory races.

OPTIONAL RACES

The optional races afford you opportunities to shop for odds. We do not recommend playing anything under 8-1 in any of these races. You should look for races with weak favorites and legitimate contenders that fit your odds range. Pass on races where the short-priced horses look solid.

Remember, the cheaper the horse, the less consistency. These races are where you can put up points and separate yourself from the field.

Tournaments are a terrific way to play while limiting your investment. A good tournament player needs to have different skills from a traditional player in order to be successful, much as you need in poker.

CHAPTER EIGHT

SPORTS WAGERING
TECHNIQUES FOR
HORSE RACING

Sports betting is one of the few forms of wagering that is similar to poker and horse racing – it features you vs. the other players.

In football, for instance, you might have two wagering options. Let's say the Houston Texans are playing the Dallas Cowboys. The Cowboys are -3, or 3 point favorites. If the Cowboys win 24-20 and you bet on the Cowboys, you win. If they win 21-20, you lose.

If the game finishes 23-20 Dallas, you push, which means no one wins. (Except the house, which gets its take).

Lines are made by Vegas oddsmakers who study the games very carefully. They are not predicting, but simply trying to create a wagering line that will produce as much action on both sides as possible.

The line will often move based on early wagers. If Cowboys fans are betting heavily, the line might go up to 4 in order to get money coming in the other way.

Whenever you make your bet, you will get that line number based on when you made the bet. If you bet it at

3 and the line later moves to 4, you still get it at 3. This obviously differs from horse racing, where your odds change based on the other wagers.

Another popular sports bet is the money line wager, where you are getting actual odds. If a team is plus-200 and you are betting them to win, you are getting 2-1 odds.

For sports gamblers moving to horse racing, these are essentially the equivalent of win bets on the ponies.

However, exotic wagers in horse racing are similar to parlays in sports. A parlay is an attempt to pick the winners of several games. This is essentially the same as playing a pick three or pick four in horse racing. But in racing, you can spread your bets to include more horses.

In both instances, your potential payoffs are based on the odds of those horses or teams. Underdogs in a parlay pay more than favorites.

The same holds true in horse racing.

The biggest adjustment for a sports bettor is understanding that your odds are not locked in; they are based on how all others wager. Once you have that figured out, you will be on your way.

CHAPTER NINE

PREMIUM HANDS IN RACING
(WHEN TO GO ALL IN)

Now that you have some understanding of odds, wagering, and how to play, there are times to shove all your chips in the middle.

Getting all your money in with pocket aces pre-flop is a dream scenario in poker. You don't always win, but you will never be behind before the flop.

In horse racing, there are several scenarios when you want to take the rubber band off the bankroll and take your swing for a big score.

Here are some of our favorite scenarios, which often arise at the track, and can happen several times a day if you are playing a multitude of tracks. They correspond to premium hands in poker. When you see these scenarios, it is time to get all your chips in the middle:

Favorable pace scenario (Pocket Aces): Pace is a critical element to handicapping horses. There is an old saying that "pace makes the race."

This is simply the most critical element to horse handicapping. Knowing which horses are likely to make the lead, which are likely to stalk and those who will come from behind is the best way to approach any race.

Map out these scenarios first, then proceed with your handicapping. A favorable pace scenario is the absolute best time to jump in with both feet and get all your chips in the middle. There is no shortage of these scenarios.

Horses can be categorized as front-runners, pace-pressers, stalkers and closers.

Front runners by definition like to be in the lead. Pace pressers like to be near the lead, pushing the pace.

Stalkers are generally just off the pace, while closers like to come from behind.

Closers often need a fast pace in front of them, so the front-runners will tire out. Failing that, a contested pace, with three or more horses dueling for the lead.

That gives us any number of favorable pace scenarios.

One such scenario might occur where there is a "Lone F" or lone front-runner in the field. Even if the horse is cheaper in class, an easy lead and an advantage in the pace is a big edge. The horse will likely get brave and keep going. As we have mentioned before, horses are by nature pack animals. They will often defer to stronger horses. A weaker horse who gets loose doesn't know there are stronger horses behind him or her. If you find this scenario, unload. These are solid plays.

Another massive pace play is a race that has several horses that are front-running, need-the-lead types, and only one confirmed closer. The front-runners will duel themselves out of contention early, leaving the closer to pick up the pieces.

Don't assume closers are better at longer races. Often, in sprints featuring faster horses, there are so many front-runners they burn out and set it up for the closers.

(By the same token, speed horses going long are often solid plays).

Closers usually don't get bet as strongly as front runners simply because they have to negotiate all of the horses in front of them. Handicappers are less likely to unload on a horse that has a lot to overcome. But if the pace sets up for them, these are strong situations to make a serious play.

The more you play, the more you will see these scenarios develop and figure out when to shove all your chips in the middle. The Lone F and Lone Closer plays are solid gold.

Always remember, Pace is critical. Once you have mastered the past performances, look for favorable pace scenarios, especially with horses that are long shots. You can also keep an eye on horses that are in unfavorable pace scenarios when they return to run next time and get one more favorable. Their last race might look terrible, but you will know why. Most handicappers are way too reliant on a horse's last race without looking at its entire body of work; make sure you look at a horse's history in terms of what they have done in certain situations, not just what they did in their last race. This will give you an edge over 80 percent of the horseplayers out there.

Track bias (Pocket Kings). It often happens where a track favors a certain type of runner. If you see the first five races at a given race track, and all five are won by horses on the lead early, what do you think is going to happen in the sixth race? In addition, some tracks develop a bias that favors horses that race on the inside portion of the track; at others the rail is a disadvantage. Basically, watch and learn and be as observant as possible. Sniffing out a bias can get you some terrific payoffs. In addition, keep notes on horses that run on days with severe biases. If a solid closer runs on a day where only front-runners win, his last race will look awful in the past performances. But you will know why, and if the horse returns to a fair track, he is more likely to run his best race again, often at a big price. Many long shots come from this; even if you are wrong about a horse once, that doesn't mean you are wrong about his overall level. Going from a biased track to a fair one (or even better, one biased in the horse's favor) will often lead to massive reversals in results, and big tickets cashed on your end.

Back in class (Ace/King): When horses have success, their trainers will often jump them up to face tougher competition. For instance, a horse races at the $5,000 claiming level and wins two races in a row. So he jumps up to $10,000 and runs poorly. They try him a second time at $10,000, and he struggles again. When the horse drops back down to a $5,000 claiming level he is often a good bet, especially if his odds are 6-1 or higher. Also, look for subsets of this scenario. A horse running in a $5,000 claimer open to any horse that moves to a $5,000 claimer for non-winners of three races is taking a huge plunge in class and facing much easier horses. By the same token, a filly running against boys for the same price tag who runs poorly will often wake up when she returns to facing females. Males do race females in thoroughbred racing, and some females (Rachel Alexandra, Zenyatta, Havre de Grace) have beaten the boys at the top levels. But in the cheaper races, where find our long shots, it doesn't happen very often. Most tracks provide enough races for fillies to run against their own kind. Sometimes, trainers will try them against the boys. When they fail and return to fillies, be prepared to bet them. In general, fillies don't beat boys very often except at the highest level. It usually goes back to the pack mentality, and fillies are often intimidated. When they get back in with their own, jump in with both hands if they have had success against fillies before.

Keep an eye on the maidens (Pocket Queens). One of the biggest class drops in horse racing is when a horse drops out of maiden allowance races into maiden claiming. Horses that take this plunge might not have shown much in their debut, but the movement to easier horses often wakes them up. This works particularly well when a horse is making his second start, since they often improve dramatically. Throw in first time Lasix, and you have a home-run scenario.

Lasix is a drug given to horses to stop them from bleeding. Horses often bleed during a race from exerting themselves. The blood goes into their lungs, making it difficult to breathe. Thus, when they get Lasix, it helps them improve. The maiden drop/second start/First Lasix angle is huge.

In addition, horses often improve dramatically in their second career start. Small equipment changes, such as the addition of blinkers, can make all the difference in the world. A horse that might have shown nothing first time out for a high-percentage trainer getting a small equipment change is worth a flyer, especially at huge odds. You can find several giant long shots doing this. Don't assume these horses won't improve. Add in a class drop and you are shoving your chips in again.

Some people are afraid to bet maiden races because the horses do not have enough of a body of work. But with these scenarios, you can find long shots, which is our primary goal. If you are scared, get a dog. Don't be afraid of these races; they can make you a lot of money.

Back on the right surface (Pocket Jacks). Because horses race on a variety of surfaces – dirt, turf and synthetic dirt – they often respond differently to each. Some horses are good on all three, but many are good at only one. Checking a horse's record on the surface is always helpful. A horse might win several races on a traditional dirt track, then struggle on synthetic or turf. Usually, returning to the favored surface leads to a return to success. Some horses are actually much better on specific tracks as well as surfaces. "Horses for courses" as they are called always bear watching. The past performances will give you each horse's record at a given track, distance and surface. Use these as important tools in your wagers.

CHAPTER TEN

ADVANCED WAGERING
TECHNIQUES

You are now armed with enough knowledge to dive in and play the races online.

If you are like most action junkies, however, you want big scores. You want to swing for the fences and attempt to collect some big returns.

If you are new to the game, these are not considered traditional bets. They are designed to get you some big scores that will pad your bankroll. They are based on some of the scenarios outlined in the previous chapter.

If you are a long time horse fan, these strategies alone are worth the price of the book. They will give you a new way to look at playing trifectas and super-fectas in particular. These are non-traditional strategies that old-time horseplayers scoff at. Newcomers will find them to be a path to monster scores.

Earlier, we discussed boxing and the cost of bets for trifectas and supers. We generally don't favor that strategy. What we do recommend is what we call the Pyramid Strategy of wagering. This allows you to use more horses, add more long shots to the wager and thus collect bigger scores.

We also use wheels and back wheels.

These strategies are not to be used on every race. There are scenarios where it works perfectly; more on that soon.

In the 2011 Kentucky Derby, our wheel strategy yielded a trifecta payoff of almost $2,000 off an outlay of $56.

Let's take a look at how we did it, and start with trifectas.

The Pyramid Strategy involves building from top to bottom. You settle in on one or two horses in first, three to four in second and as many as possible in third.

You are essentially building a pyramid out of numbers, with the base line (third) having the most horses. This enables you to narrow down the potential winner, yet use more long shots in second and third.

A Pyramid ticket might look like this:

1-2
With
1-2-3-4
With
1-2-3-4-5-6

This ticket, for a $1 bet, costs the same as a four-horse box ($24).

Look at the advantage; if you narrow the top of your ticket to just two horses, you can now have the same four in second, plus an additional two horses in third.

You have given yourself more opportunities to win by using more horses simply by handicapping better.

If you can narrow it even further to one horse on top, you can include the entire field on the bottom and try to catch an extreme longshot (and nice payoff).

When this works: This is especially useful in races where you have some of the scenarios outlined in the last chapter, specifically the favorable pace scenario. Singling in on the lone closer in a field full of speed can often lead to the beginning of a nice payoff.

You should not play these bets with the first two favorites on top, or in races where there appear to be three standouts and they are all taking wagering action. What you really want is a race where the favorites are vulnerable, and your top pyramid horses are at least 5-1.

The wheel (technically called a part wheel) strategy is similar but involves singling in on one horse. Again, this is particularly useful when you have any of the scenarios from the prior chapter and your horse offers value in the win pool.

In this strategy, you pyramid your horse in first, like this:

1
With
2-3-4
With
2-3-4-5-6

The cost is $12. Then you put your horse in second:

2-3-4
With
1
With 2-3-4-5-6

Your total cost is just $24, and you now have some coverage with your horse in case he doesn't win.

This is a nice way to pick up some serious scores, especially if you have some big-priced horses on the bottom of your ticket and a favorite outside the top three. This is the strategy we used to hit the 2011 Derby trifecta.

The pyramid/wheeling strategy works extremely well for superfectas as well. There is an old saying for super players: "Anyone can run fourth." And that is often true.

Again, a five-horse super box costs you $120 for a $1 ticket. But look at the value in the pyramid, playing an inexpensive ticket that gives you several options.

This is one that can be played very cheaply:

1
With
2-3
With
2-3-4
With
2-3-4-5

This is just $8. You can also put the 1 horse in second, and add the 2 horse in first, all for much less than ($13) the $24 you used to box four horses.

You don't need all four horses to run their race. You can also add many more horses and spend a huge amount of money for some big scores.

Here is the good news, however, if you want to play for a smaller dollar amount and limit your bankroll risks to a more reasonable investment. If you want to play the 10 cent superfecta, you can include a massive number of horses for under $20. Check out this pyramid concept that could get you a huge score:

1-2
With
1-2-3-4
With
1-2-3-4-5-6

With
1-2-3-4-5-6-7-8-9-10

That little beauty will cost you $168 for a dollar. But you can bet the dime super for just $16.80. (Not all tracks offer 10 cent supers).

Of course, you have to stick to the 5-1 or higher on the top, and hopefully leave the favorite out of the second slot as well. This will often lead to some scores in the $100-$200 range for 10 cents; $1-2K minimum for $168.

In a 10-horse field, you would have the entire field in fourth, and you are hoping for a massive long shot. This isn't all wishful thinking; it doesn't take much for a hopeless horse to clunk up for fourth and blow up the superfecta. If the favorite runs a bad race, you are cashing big.

These strategies work best in the following circumstances:

1. Cheaper races with horses that aren't very good.
2. Big, wide open fields.
3. Fields with a false betting favorite.
4. Fields where you have one of our five scenarios.

These bets simply don't work well in short fields or if you are using the favorite on top. Your potential return is simply never enough to justify your risk. Remember, you are looking for value in your high-risk, high-reward bets. Never create high-risk, no-reward bets.

Sometimes you will get the worst-case scenario, where your 5-1 wins, a 3-1 runs second, the favorite comes in third and another mid-odds horse runs fourth. You aren't going to make much money. But when you get something like 5-1, 10-1, 15-1 and 40-1, you can ship it.

Now, for those of you who want to go for a massive score, we offer what we call the Reverse Pyramid or Reverse Wheel strategy.

This is a bet that requires the same four scenarios as above, plus these:

1. Your key horse has to be 10-1 or higher.
2. You need a closer
3. You need a horse that has few wins, but hits the board at a high percentage and has run second or third in the bulk of his career races.

This is a strategy that old-timers will scoff at, but it can lead to massive scores.

Some horses simply don't like to win. They always run well enough to get a piece of the purse, but they never get all the way on top. It goes back to the pack mentality we discussed before.

For instance, let's pretend we have a horse named Spunky Manker. He is 15-1 on the morning line, and is racing in his 51st career race. His career record: 50 starts, 3 wins, 15 seconds and 20 thirds.

Spunky is a closer who also has finished fourth four times.

He has only three wins in 50 starts, but here is a stat poker players will love – he has finished second or third 70 percent of the time in his career. Because he is a closer, he is less likely to get bet.

Spunky is exactly the kind of horse we love to play, especially online. These horses are very common and they offer solid value. Let's take a look:

Spunky is the No. 1 horse. In our reverse bet, we are going to key Spunky in second and third in a trifecta. Our bet would look like this:

2-3-4
With
1
With
2-3-4-5-6-7-8-9-10

That puts Spunky in second. Now, let's do something that might seem completely bizarre, but we will also key him in the third spot of the trifecta, using the same horses first and second. We are essentially gambling that Spunky is good enough to run as he has 70 percent of his career, but not really good enough to win.

This is how that ticket would look:

2-3-4
With
2-3-4-5-6-7-8-9-10
With
1

This strategy may seem odd, but it has produced some incredible payoffs, especially when the favorite is not one of the horses on top. If you get a decent-priced horse (10-1 or higher on top), and Spunky can clunk up for third or second, you can get a nice score. Using all ten horses in the bet will give you a shot at a massive payoff.

Yes, occasionally Spunky will jump up and win a race.

But poker players will understand the logic; your play is based on the 70 percent chance he will run how he always does, versus a 6 percent chance he wins and a 24 percent chance he misses the board.

Your odds are 70 percent vs. the 30 percent chance he runs first or fourth or worse. If you can get your chips in on those odds, you have a great chance to win.

This strategy has been widely dismissed by serious handicappers, but used properly it can create huge scores, and it gives players an edge by using a ticket most traditionalists would not. (We once hit an $11k trifecta at Oaklawn Park using this strategy).

This is a poker-based strategy that can revolutionize the way you play trifectas and superfectas. If you are a longtime horse player, monitor a few of these scenarios and see how they play out before you actually try it. You will be stunned at how often it is an effective strategy.

For online junkies who advance past the basics, we love these strategies for trifectas and superfectas. Our other preferred wagers are pick threes and pick fours.

As far as pick thee and pick four wagers, we outlined earlier how we spread our bets to try to pick up nice scores. However, here are some more specific rules that will help you determine whether or not to play these bets and how to keep them affordable.

PICK THREE/FOUR

Picking the winner of three straight races by using just one horse in each race is not very viable. Usually, the horses you are using are favorites, and the rare times you hit won't pay you much. But if you follow these rules and spend a little more money, you can pick up some nice scores:

Never single a horse that is odds-on (less than even money). If you can't beat that horse, don't bother with the pick 3. For a legitimate payoff, you need to beat horses like that. If you think you can, go that way. If not, pass.

If you are spreading deep in a race, make sure you

have a legitimate chance to beat the favorite. There is nothing worse than using six or seven horses in a wide-open race and seeing a 2-1 shot romp home.

Make a stand. Somewhere, you will need to step up and make a stand in the pick three. That might mean singling a horse that isn't the favorite (look for one of our five scenarios) or only going with two horses in one race. Do your handicapping and don't be afraid to gamble that you are right.

Don't scrimp if you are unsure. If you have a six horse field and are using five horses, throw in the sixth unless he has three legs.

These same strategies apply to the pick four, although No. 3 is more critical because the cost of the ticket is higher.

For all of these bets, try to keep the following guidelines in mind:

Think big. While you can't figure out the returns, make sure you have enough long shots in your bet to justify the cost. If you aren't aiming for at least a 10-1 return on investment for a tri, super or pick three, don't bother. Stick with win wagering.

The favorites are not your friends. Sometimes you can get a big score when they win, but it's rare. Focus on the big score. We like our key/pyramid horses on top to be AT LEAST 5-1, preferably higher. Focus on the 67 percent of the time when the favorite doesn't win. It is OK in a pick four to have one favorite, but if you think more than one will win, you should pass.

This is the No. 1 rule of being an online action junkie or a gambler of any kind, and you have already seen it once in this book: "If you are scared, get a dog." Fear has no place in gambling. A scared player will lose, plain and simple. Develop a bankroll, stick to it and play within it. But never bet just enough to lose. Trifectas and supers can be tricky; if you don't feel like all your bases are covered, fold the cards.

Remember the five scenarios. These are your pocket aces, kings, queens, jacks and Big Slick. That is when you want to step out and take a major swing at the fences.

If you lose a race, don't be afraid to go back and look at the race again. Were you wrong? What did you miss? Sometimes you don't miss anything, and you played it perfectly. But your aces got cracked. It happens.

Using these strategies in concert with our five dream scenarios will make your online horse career a success-ful one.

Calculating the cost of your wagers is a big key to staying within your bankroll. There is no shortage of places where you can do this.

Of course, we are here to help.

You can use the following tables to calculate the cost of all of your exotic wagers. This will give you an idea of how much your bet will cost you. These tables are courtesy of our friends at Sam Houston Race Park.

In addition, there are several free online wager

calculators. You can also punch your bets in online without confirming them on most sites to see what a tri, super, pick three or pick four combination would cost you.

Following are the tables for all the key bets, which will allow you to determine your costs before you decide on a final wager:

QUINELLA WHEEL AND BOX COSTS
Based on a $2 wager

1 horse with	Wheel cost	No. of horses	Box cost
2 others	$4	3	$6
3 others	$6	4	$12
4 others	$8	5	$20
5 others	$10	6	$30
6 others	$12	7	$42
7 others	$14	8	$56
8 others	$16	9	$72
9 others	$18	10	$90
10 others	$20	11	$110
11 others	$22	12	$132

EXACTA WHEEL AND BOX COSTS

Based on a $2 wager

1 horse with	Wheel cost	No. of horses	Box cost
2 others	$4	2	$4
3 others	$6	3	$12
4 others	$8	4	$24
5 others	$10	5	$40
6 others	$12	6	$60
7 others	$14	7	$84
8 others	$16	8	$112
9 others	$18	9	$144
10 others	$20	10	$180
11 others	$22	11	$220
		12	$264

TRIFECTA WHEEL AND BOX COSTS

Based on a $1 wager

1 horse with	Wheel cost	No. of horses	Box cost
2 others	$4	3	$6
3 others	$6	4	$24
4 others	$12	5	$60
5 others	$20	6	$120
6 others	$30	7	$210
7 others	$42	8	$336
8 others	$56	9	$504
9 others	$72	10	$720
10 others	$90	11	$990
11 others	$110	12	$1320

SUPERFECTA WHEEL AND BOX COSTS
Based on a $1 wager

1 horse with	Wheel cost	No. of horses	Box cost
3 others	$6	4	$24
4 others	$24	5	$120
5 others	$60	6	$360
6 others	$120	7	$840
7 others	$210	8	$1,680
8 others	$336	9	$3,024
9 others	$504	10	$5,040
10 others	$720	11	$7,920
11 others	$990	12	$11,880

CONCLUSION

So now you are armed with the basics. You have some strategies that will work to pull big scores. You have begun your transition from poker or sports betting to horse racing.

There is much to learn, but you have taken a huge first step. It's time to let go of Black Friday and find a new game. Horse racing provides all the action, a chance to compete against others, even tournaments.

And it can all be done completely legally.

You now have pocket aces, and it's time to go all-in on horse racing.

GLOSSARY OF RACING TERMS

Here are some terms that might come up at the track:

AGE: The age of a horse; all horses officially become a year older on Jan.1 regardless of their actual birthday.

ALLOWANCE: A type of race for quality horses.

ALSO-RAN: A horse who finishes out of the money.

BREAK MAIDEN: Horse wins its first race of its career.

CLAIMING: Type of race where a horse is entered for a selling price.

CLOSER: A horse that comes from off the pace.

COLT: Male horse under 5 years of age.

COUPLED: Two or more horses running as a single entry from a betting perspective, such as 1 and 1A.

DAILY DOUBLE: Type of wager where the gambler picks the winners of two consecutive races.

DEAD-HEAT: Two or more horses finishing in a tie at the wire.

DISQUALIFICATION: When the order of finished is changed because of a rules violation.

DISTAFF: A female horse or race for a female horse.

EXACTA: Selecting the first two finishers in a race in exact order.

FIELD: The horses in a race.

FILLY: Female horse through the end of their 4-year-old year. Fillies usually run against their own kind, although sometimes they race the boys.

FRACTIONAL TIME: Intermediate time recorded in a race, as at the quarter, half, etc.

FRONT-RUNNER: A horse who prefers to lead the field in the early stages.

FURLONG: One-eighth of a mile (220 yards).

HANDICAPPER: A person who makes selections for races.

HEAD: A margin between horses (the length of his head).

INQUIRY: Reviewing a race for possible rules infractions.

JUVENILE: Two-year-old horse.

LASIX: A drug that helps horses deal with bleeding issues.

MAIDEN: A horse who has not won a race.

MARE: Female horse 5 years old or older.

MORNING LINE: Projected odds before wagering begins.

NECK: Form of measuring; the length of a horse's neck.

NOSE: Form of measuring; the smallest a horse can win by.

ODDS ON: Odds of less than even money.

ON THE BOARD: Finishing in the top three.

ON THE NOSE: Betting a horse to win.

PARIMUTUEL: A form of wagering in which all money bet is divided up among those who have winning tickets.

PAST PERFORMANCES: A collection of data that represents a horse's history.

PHOTO FINISH: A result so close a camera is needed to determine the result.

PICK SIX: A wager in which the winners of six consecutive races must be selected.

POST TIME: Designated time for a race to start.

PURSE: Prize money for a horse race.

QUINELLA: Bet in which first two finishers must be picked in either order.

ROUTE: A race of a mile or longer.

SHOW: Third position at the finish; also a bet to run third.

SPRINT: A race shorter than a mile.

STAKE: A race for the best horses.

STRETCH: Final portion of the racetrack to the finish line.

SUPERFECTA: Picking the first four finishers in exact order.

TRACK BIAS: A surface that favors a running style or position.

TRIFECTA: Picking the first three finishers in exact order.

Email Fred Faour: acingracing@yahoo.com
You can also follow him on Twitter @fredfaour

CPSIA information can be obtained
at www.ICGtesting.com
Printed in the USA
LVOW07s2256140517
534528LV00009B/374/P